WHATEVER IT TAKES™

A JOURNEY INTO THE HEART OF HUMAN ACHIEVEMENT™

BY BOB MOAWAD

DESIGNED BY KOBI YAMADA AND STEVE POTTER

THOUGHTS TO INSPIRE AND CELEBRATE
YOUR COMMITMENT TO EXCELLENCE™

COM·PEN´·DI·UM™
INCORPORATED

PUBLISHING & COMMUNICATIONS
SEATTLE, WASHINGTON

ACKNOWLEDGEMENTS

The quotations in this book were gathered lovingly but unscientifically over several years and/or contributed by many friends and clients. Some arrived— and survived in our files—on scraps of paper and may therefore be imperfectly worded or attributed. Those that are attributed as "Keynotes" were drawn from the EDGE Keynote cards, 30 million of which have already been circulated throughout the world. To the authors, contributors and original sources, our thanks, and where appropriate, our apologies. –The editors.

ABOUT EDGE LEARNING INSTITUTE

For information on the worldwide programs conducted by Bob Moawad and the EDGE Learning Institute, call toll free 800-858-1484 or 800-682-2603.

WITH SPECIAL THANKS TO

Dick Anderson, Bill Cole, Maren Ellingson, Nancy Geier, Dennis Goin, Andrew Bennett, Skip Wilkins, Pat Gaddis, Sandy Jameson, Debbie Zak, Andrea Moawad, Bob Moawad, Jr., Trevor Moawad, Ron Perry and the rest of the team at EDGE Learning Institute.

CREDITS

Edited by Dan Zadra and Katie Lambert.
Designed by Kobi Yamada and Steve Potter.

Printed in Hong Kong

A CALL TO EXCELLENCE

Long before the sun has risen or the people who deliver
your morning newspaper have completed their rounds,
millions of people are already wide-awake. Perhaps like you,
they are restlessly and relentlessly pursuing their dreams.

Some are corporate executives, well-known celebrities,
athletes, coaches, officials or leaders. But most are our
neighbors, friends, relatives, employees or co-workers:
The carpenter checking his tools; the sales manager packing
her bags; the small business owner running spreadsheets on
the kitchen computer; the teacher creating banners for the
school assembly; the student athlete doing push-ups by his
bed. The light is on in their windows, minds and hearts.

These are first-rate people in action—excellence, plain and simple. By doing whatever it takes to become the best they are capable of becoming, they lift our spirits. They stretch our boundaries. They energize our communities. And they bring new meaning to the terms, "job well-done" and "life well-led." Because you share that spirit, this book is dedicated to you.

Positively,

Bob Moawad

THE GIFT

The best day of your life is the one on which you decide your life is your own. No apologies or excuses. No one to lean on, rely on, or blame.
The gift of life is yours—it is an amazing journey—and you alone are responsible for the quality of it. This is the day your life really begins.

What is life for?
It is for you.
−ABRAHAM MASLOW

Something wonderful, something hidden. A gift unique to you. Find it.

—EMERSON

❖

For awhile I looked outside to see what I could make the world give me, instead of looking inside to see what was there.

—BELL LIVINGSTONE

❖

People talk about "finding" their lives. In reality, your life is not something you find—it's something you create.

—DAVID PHILLIPS

THE GIFT

The greatest thing is, at any moment, to be willing to give up who we are in order to become all that we can become.

—MAX DE PREE

◇

I was restless. I was doing okay, but I was restless. One day it dawned on me that I had been looking at life through the wrong end of the telescope. It was up to me to turn it around— to make it bigger, better, more satisfying.

—ARNOLD SWARZENEGGER

◇

Nothing is the worst thing that can happen to us.

—RICHARD BACH

**You don't need
to be sick to get better.**

—DICK ANDERSON

◇

**That's what freedom is all about—
a chance to be better.**

—ALBERT CAMUS

◇

**It's your life, your one and only life—
so take excellence *very* personally.**

—SCOTT JOHNSON

THE GIFT

9

**Champions are born...
and then unmade.**

—CONVERSE

◇

**Don't be afraid to give
up the good to go for the great.**

—KENNY ROGERS

◇

**You only live once—but if you work
it right, once is enough.**

—JOE E. LEWIS

THE GIFT

"Is life worth living?"
The question does not make any sense.
—ERICH FROMM

◇

In the Auschwitz death camp,
a group of inmates told Victor Frankl
that they no longer expected anything
from life. Frankl responded that they
had it backward. "Life expects something of you, and it is up to
every individual to discover
what it should be."

◇

Life is ours to be spent,
not saved.
—D. H. LAWRENCE

Begin doing what you want to do now. We are not living in eternity. We have only this moment, sparkling like a star in our hand— and melting like a snowflake.

—MARIE BEYNON RAY

◇

One of these days is none of these days.

—ENGLISH PROVERB

◇

No, you never get any fun out of the things you haven't done.

—OGDEN NASH

Neglect not the gift that is in thee.

—NEW TESTAMENT

◇

I wouldn't miss life for anything!

—ANNE WILSON SHAEF

◇

Alas for those who never sing but die with all their music in them.

—OLIVER WENDELL HOLMES

THE GIFT

THE FREEDOM

Allow yourself the freedom to grow and expand.

Form the habit of saying yes to your own potential.

Take time to think of all the

reasons why you can and why

you will excel at something

*It's not who we are
that holds us back, it's
who we think we're not.*

—MICHAEL NOLAN

wonderful…because there will always be plenty of

people around to tell you why you can't.

Discover your possibilities.

—Dr. Robert Schuller

◇

**The greatest crime in the world
is not developing your potential.
When you do what you do best,
you are helping not only
yourself, but the world.**

—Roger Williams

◇

**You don't get to choose how or
when you're going to die. You can only
decide how you're going to live. Now.**

—Joan Baez

THE FREEDOM

**If we did all the things
we are capable of, we would literally
astound ourselves.**

—THOMAS EDISON

◇

**Help! I'm being held "prisoner" by my
heredity and environment.**

—DENNIS ALLEN

◇

**It's not trespassing if the boundaries
you cross are your own.**

—JOHNNY WALKER

THE FREEDOM

Caution! The left-brained
world wants you to "be realistic"...
"quit dreaming"..."get your head out
of the clouds"..."get your feet on the
ground"...and "be just like us."
To advance and prosper,
steadfastly ignore that advice.

—MARILYN GREY

◇

There has never been another you.
With no effort on your part you were
born to be something very special and
set apart. What you are going to do
in appreciation of that gift is a
decision only you can make.

—DAN ZADRA

They say you can't do it, but sometimes that doesn't always work.

—CASEY STENGEL

◇

If you're strong enough, there are no precedents.

—F. SCOTT FITZGERALD

◇

Be faithful to that which exists nowhere but in yourself.

—ANDRE GIDE

THE FREEDOM

**Anytime you poke your head
above the crowd, someone will
take a poke at it.**
—UNITED TECHNOLOGIES

◇

**Just remember that you don't
have to be what they want you to be.**
—MUHAMMAD ALI

◇

**To be nobody but yourself
in a world which is doing its best,
day and night, to make you like everybody else is to fight the hardest battle
which any human being can fight...**
but never stop fighting!
—E. E. CUMMINGS

If you truly expect to realize your dreams, abandon the need for blanket approval. If conforming to everyone else's expectations is the number one goal, you have sacrificed your uniqueness and, therefore, your excellence.

—DON WARD

◇

Most of our limitations are self-imposed. Roger Bannister was the first human to run a sub-four-minute mile—a barrier that was previously deemed insurmountable. Immediately after Bannister proved it was "possible," runners all over the world repeated his feat.

—BOB MOAWAD

THE FREEDOM

20

Never tell a young person that something cannot be done. God may have waited centuries for someone ignorant enough of the impossible to do that very thing.

—Dr. J. R. Holmes

◇

Records are set all the time by big-hearted people who don't have the right background, ability or experience—or who simply don't know any better.

—Kobi Yamada

◇

Remember always that you not only have the right to be an individual, you have an obligation to be one.

—Eleanor Roosevelt

THE FREEDOM

THE DREAM

Dreams are the picture-making power of your imagination. They are the stuff of which life, hope, love, fun, accomplishment and excellence

Imagination is the preview of life's coming attractions.
—LARRY EISENBERG

are made. All great things are born there. Respect and nurture your dreams—believe in them—and bring them to the sunshine and the light.

**Keep true to the
dreams of thy youth.**

—JOHANN FRIEDRICH VON SCHILLER

◇

**At least once a day,
allow yourself the freedom to
think and dream for yourself.**

—ALBERT EINSTEIN

◇

**Most of us are so busy
doing what we think we have to do,
that we do not think about what
we really want to do.**

—ROBERT PERCIVAL

THE DREAM

"Why not?" is a slogan
for an interesting life.

—MASON COOLEY

◇

You have to think anyway,
so why not think big?

—DONALD TRUMP

◇

We can only thrive when we have a
goal—a passionate purpose which bears
upon the public interest.

—MARGARET E. KUHN

THE DREAM

**Believe it! High expectations are
the key to everything.**

—SAM WALTON

◇

**Most people don't aim too high and
miss, they aim too low and hit.**

—BOB MOAWAD

◇

**Is not life a hundred times
too short for us to bore ourselves?**

—FRIEDRICH NIETZSCHE

THE DREAM

Your dreams are not meant to put you to sleep, but to alert and arouse you to your immense possibilities.
—DAVID PHILLIPS

◇

**You're damn right it's possible.
If you dreamed it up, it's possible.
You're the only person who can say,
"It's impossible."**
—CARLO MENTA

◇

Extraordinary people visualize not what is possible or probable, but rather what is impossible. And by visualizing the impossible, they begin to see it as possible.
—CHERIE CARTER-SCOTT

THE DREAM

Those who dream by night awake
to find that it was vanity. But the
dreamers of day are dangerous; they
may act out their dreams with open
eyes to make it possible.

—T. E. LAWRENCE

◇

Always dream and shoot
higher than you know you can do.
Don't bother just to be better than
your contemporaries or predecessors.
Try to be better than yourself.

—WILLIAM FAULKNER

THE DREAM

27

**The prize goes to the person
who sees the future the quickest.**

—WILLIAM STIRITZ

◇

**There are two worlds: The world
that we can measure with line and rule,
and the world we feel with our hearts
and imaginations.**

—LEIGH HUNT

◇

**The man who has
no imagination has no wings.**

—MUHAMMAD ALI

THE DREAM

**Dreams are what get you started.
Discipline is what keeps you going.**

—JIM RYAN

◇

**We must teach our children
to dream with open eyes.**

—HARRY EDWARDS

◇

**Forever be a dreamer!
When your memories outnumber
your dreams, the end is near.**

—EDGE KEYNOTE

THE DREAM

THE GOAL

You don't have to take life the way it comes to you.

By converting your dreams into goals, and your goals into plans, you can design your life to come to you the way you want it. You can live your life on purpose, instead of by chance.

A goal is a dream with its feet on the ground.

—FRANK VIZARRE

**A dream without a goal
is just a wish.**

—BILL COLE

◇

**It takes as much energy to wish
as it does to plan.**

—ELEANOR ROOSEVELT

◇

**Concentrate on finding your goal,
then concentrate on reaching it.**

—MICHAEL FRIEDSAM

THE GOAL

If you don't know where you're going,
how will you know when you get there?

—CASEY STENGEL

◇

People are like guided missiles.
Without a target, they wander
aimlessly across the horizon and
eventually self-destruct.

—EDGE KEYNOTE

◇

There is only one success—to be able to
spend your life in your own way.

—CHRISTOPHER MORLEY

THE GOAL

32

**The best way to
predict the future is to invent it.**

—ALAN KAY

◇

**The world is before you,
and you need not take it or leave it
as it was when you came in.**

—JAMES BALDWIN

◇

**Planning is bringing the future
into the present so that you can do
something about it now.**

—ALAN LAKEIN

The world stands aside to let anyone pass who knows where he is going.

—DAVID JORDAN

◇

What do you want to do? What do you want to be? What do you want to have? Where do you want to go? Who do you want to go with? How the hell do you plan to get there? Write it down. Go do it. Enjoy it. Share it. It doesn't get much simpler or better than that.

—LEE IACOCCA

◇

Decide to love and do what you like.

—ST. AUGUSTINE

THE GOAL

**Progress comes from caring
more about what needs to be done
than about who gets the credit.**
—DOROTHY HEIGHT

◇

**Goals give purpose.
Purpose gives faith. Faith gives
courage. Courage gives enthusiasm.
Enthusiasm gives energy. Energy gives
life. Life lifts you over the bar.**
—BOB RICHARDS, POLE VAULTER

◇

**When we set exciting worth-
while goals for ourselves, they work
in two ways: We work on them,
and they work on us.**
—BOB MOAWAD

THE GOAL

**Dreams whet your appetite,
but goals make you hungry.**

—JOSIE BISSETT

◇

**We all love big ideas.
If an organization lacks enthusiasm,
if the people are bored, it's time for a
big idea. The moment you set a new
goal, you create a gap between where
you are and where you really
want to be. The urge to close that
gap generates tension, energy,
enthusiasm, purpose and drive.**

—HARRY GRAY

THE GOAL

**Set exciting personal goals.
You will live longer.**

—BOB MOAWAD

◈

**Keep changing,
because when you're through
changing—you're through.**

—BERT-OLAF SVANHOLM

◈

**Two roads diverged in a wood, and I—
I took the one less traveled by,
And that has made all the difference.**

—ROBERT FROST

THE PLUNGE

Indecision and second-guessing are the mortal enemies of spontaneous brilliance and planning. Without action, your dream, goal or plan has little meaning in the world.

Sometimes you just have to take the leap, and build your wings on the way down.

—KOBI YAMADA

Living and risking are close companions. If you sense that you have made a good decision, have faith. Move forward.

A life not put to the test
is not worth living.

—EPICTECUS

❖

Courage is the capacity to confront
what can be imagined.

—LEO ROSTEN

❖

You must get involved to have
an impact. No one is impressed with
the won–lost record of the referee.

—JOHN HOLCOMB

THE PLUNGE

There's as much risk in doing nothing as in doing something.

—TRAMMELL CROW

◇

Action without planning is fatal, but planning without action is futile.

—TRACIE VAN EIMEREN

◇

If you put everything off till you're sure of it, you'll get nothing done.

—NORMAN VINCENT PEALE

THE PLUNGE

**You cannot lead
where you do not go.**

—EDGE KEYNOTE

◇

**If you don't execute your ideas...
they'll die.**

—ROBERT PERCIVAL

◇

**A year from now you will wish
you had started today.**

—KAREN LAMB

THE PLUNGE

**If you have a dream,
give it a chance to happen.**

—RICH DEVOS

◆

**Sometimes you just have
to trust your intuition.**

—WILLIAM GATES, MICROSOFT

◆

**We wouldn't worry nearly as much
about what others thought of us, if we
recognized how seldom they did.**

—EDGE KEYNOTE

**If you're going to worry, don't do it.
If you do it, don't worry.**

—EDGE KEYNOTE

◇

**Action may not always bring happiness,
but there is no happiness without action.**

—BENJAMIN DISRAELI

◇

**The moment you commit and quit
holding back, all sorts of unforeseen
incidents, meetings and material
assistance will rise up to help you.
The simple act of commitment is
a powerful magnet for help.**

—NAPOLEON HILL

THE PLUNGE

There comes a moment when you have to stop revving up the car and shove it into gear.

—DAVID MAHONEY

◆

You miss 100 percent of the shots you never take.

—WAYNE GRETZKY, PRO HOCKEY PLAYER

◆

Just do it.

—NIKE

THE PLUNGE

**I'd rather be sorry for something
I did than for something I didn't do.**

—RED SCOTT

◇

**Be not the slave of your own past—
plunge into the sublime seas, dive deep,
and swim far, so you shall come back
with self-respect, with new power, with
an advanced experience that shall
explain and overlook the old.**

—EMERSON

◇

**The saddest words of tongue or pen are
these four words—it might have been.**

—OLIVER WENDELL HOLMES

THE PLUNGE

THE MISTAKES

Fail forward! Whenever you undertake a new project, attempt to make as many mistakes as rapidly as possible

Test fast, fail fast, adjust fast.

—TOM PETERS

in order to learn as much as you can in the shortest period of time. Mistakes are great. Learn from them; research them; use them to propel you forward.

**If at first you don't succeed,
you're in great company.**
—ELDEN PETERSON

◇

**Jockey Eddie Arcaro lost his first 45
races. Michael Jordan was cut from his
high school basketball team. You will not
be remembered for the number of times you
failed in the beginning, but for the number
of times you succeeded in the end.**
—EDGE KEYNOTE

◇

**If you get off to a bad start,
don't worry. It's the finish not the
start that counts.**
—EDGE KEYNOTE

THE MISTAKES

How do I work? I grope.

—ALBERT EINSTEIN

◇

**Results? Why, man,
I have gotten a lot of results.
I know several thousand things
that won't work.**

—THOMAS EDISON

◇

**Those who never made a mistake
probably never made a discovery.**

—SAMUEL SMILES

THE MISTAKES

**Error is only the opportunity
to begin again, more intelligently.**

—HENRY FORD

◈

**Most of my advances
were by mistake. You uncover what is
when you get rid of what isn't.**

—BUCKMINSTER FULLER

◈

**A mistake is simply another
way of doing things.**

—KATHARINE GRAHAM

THE MISTAKES

**No more mistakes
and you're through.**

—JOHN KLEISS

◇

**If you demand perfection of
yourself, you'll seldom achieve it.
Fear of making a mistake is the
biggest single cause of making one.
Instead of pushing for perfection,
relax and pursue excellence.**

—BUD WINTER, TRACK COACH

◇

**A mistake only proves that
someone stopped talking long
enough to do something.**

—MICHAEL LEBOEUF

THE MISTAKES

**The fastest way to succeed
is to double your failure rate.**
—THOMAS J. WATSON

❖

**Critics hang around and wait
for others to make mistakes. But the
real doers of the world have no time for
criticizing others. They're too busy
doing, making mistakes, improving,
making progress.**
—DR. WAYNE DYER

❖

**Life is like playing the violin solo
in public and learning the instrument
as you go along.**
—SAMUEL BUTLER

THE MISTAKES

**For God's sake give me
someone who has brains enough
to make a fool of himself.**
—ROBERT LOUIS STEVENSON

❖

**Quit sitting up there in the bleachers.
Come on down on the field. Suit up!
Roll around in the dirt! Take a chance
on missing a pass, fumbling the ball or
making a jackass out of yourself. That's
what the champions are willing to do.**
—MISTAKES ARE GREAT

❖

**Mistakes are evidence that
you're human—and what's wrong
with being human?**
—EDGE KEYNOTE

THE MISTAKES

**Mistakes are part
of the dues one pays for a full life.**

—SOPHIA LOREN

◇

**If all else fails, immortality can always
be assured by spectacular error.**

—JOHN KENNETH GALBRAITH

◇

**In the end, there are no mistakes.
There is only yearning and learning.**

—DAN ZADRA

THE MISTAKES

THE PASSION

If you love what you do, and you feel that it matters,

then the passion will show.

In today's world, "I care" is

not just a nice phrase—it's

a two-word recipe for excellence,

success and fulfillment. It all boils down to those who really

care and those who really don't.

People who never get carried away should be.

—MALCOLM FORBES

Don't care what others think of
what you do; but care very much
about what you think you do.

—St. Frances DeSalles

◇

Caring is a powerful
business advantage.

—Scott Johnson

◇

Passion persuades.

—Anita Roddick, Body Shop

THE PASSION

Nothing splendid was ever created in cold blood. Heat is required to forge anything. Every great accomplishment is the story of a flaming heart.

—ARNOLD GLASOW

◇

Intensity for immensity.

—RUSSELL JONES

◇

Success is never the result of spontaneous combustion. You must set yourself on fire.

—ARNOLD GLASOW

THE PASSION

I believe that a person ought to know
what he believes, why he believes it,
and then believe it.
—CHARLES "TREMENDOUS" JONES

◇

How to never work
another day in your life:
Fall in love with what you do;
believe in what you're doing;
strive to continuously improve.
—BOB MOAWAD

◇

When you truly believe in something,
and you carry it in your heart, you accept
no excuses, only results.
—KEN BLANCHARD

Dedication to excellence
on any level, in any area, requires
an intensity of emotional investment.
Unfortunately, there are scores of people
who do not make the investment—who
do not feel strongly about anything.

—THEODORE ISAAC RUBIN

◇

Be fanatics. When it comes
to being, doing and dreaming
the best, be maniacs.

—A. M. ROSENTHAL

◇

I realized a long time ago that a belief
which does not spring from a conviction
in the emotions is no belief at all.

—EVELYN SCOTT

THE PASSION

58

**No matter how long I live there
will never be a dull moment.**

—HARRIET DOERR

◇

**I never went to work,
I always went to play.**

—WILLIE STARGELL, PRO BASEBALL PLAYER

◇

**There ain't no rules around here.
We're trying to accomplish something.**

—THOMAS EDISON

THE PASSION

**Pressure is neither good nor bad.
You can convert pressure into negative
tension and worry—or positive
expectation and enthusiasm.
It's a choice you make yourself.**
—EDGE KEYNOTE

◇

If you feel happy, tell your face.
—STEVE POTTER

◇

**While designing Apple Computer's
new Macintosh, Stephen Jobs flew a
pirate flag over his building to signify
his team's determination to blow all
rival teams out of the water.**
—INSIGHTS ON TEAMWORK

THE PASSION

There is only one big thing—desire.
And before it, when it is big, all is little.

—WILLA CATHER

◆

If I had to nominate a driving force in
my life, I'd plump for passion every time.
My passionate belief is that business can
be fun, it can be conducted with love
and a powerful force for good.

—ANITA RODDICK, BODY SHOP

◆

Go put your creed into your deed.

—EMERSON

THE PASSION

THE COMMITMENT

Anybody can quit. It's exactly what your adversaries or competitors hope you will do, and there's always a legitimate excuse. But have faith; hang in there. Stay in touch with your dream and commitment.

Remember that your resources are always far deeper and far greater than you ever imagine them to be. You got yourself this far. Down deep you've got what it takes to go the distance.

There are no gold medal for the 95-yard dash.

—MAX DE PREE

**Folks, we're going on a journey.
On this journey we will carry our
wounded and shoot the dissenters.**

—REENGINERING THE CORPORATION

◆

**To finish first,
you must first finish.**

—RICK MEARS

◆

**Commitment is the stuff character
is made of; the power to change the
face of things. It is the daily triumph
of integrity over skepticism.**

—UNKNOWN

THE COMMITMENT

**To be a champion
you have to believe in yourself
when no one else will.**

—SUGAR RAY ROBINSON

◆

**Ignore people who say
it can't be done.**

—ELAINE RIDEOUT

◆

**Others can stop you temporarily.
Only you can do it permanently.**

—EDGE KEYNOTE

THE COMMITMENT

**Only when I fall
do I get up again.**

—VINCENT VAN GOGH

◆

**In times of difficulty, you may
feel that your problems will go on and
on, but they won't. Every mountain has
a top. Every problem has a life span.
The question is, who is going to give in
first, the frustration or you?**

—DR. ROBERT SCHULLER

◆

**Problems come and go.
I'm in it for the long haul.**

—GEORGE BURNS

THE COMMITMENT

**The biggest enemy is doubt.
If you don't believe in what you are
doing, you aren't going to make it.**

—PHILIPPE KAHN

◇

**I attribute my success to this:
I never gave or took an excuse.**

—FLORENCE NIGHTINGALE

◇

**The great question is not
whether you have failed, but whether
you are content with failure.**

—WILLIAM SHAKESPEARE

THE COMMITMENT

We are all faced with a
series of great opportunities brilliantly
disguised as unsolvable problems.

—JOHN W. GARDNER

◇

Faith and doubt are both
needed—not as antagonists, but
working side by side—to take us
around the unknown curve.

—LILLIAN SMITH

◇

What is defeat? Nothing but
education, nothing but the first step
toward something better.

—WENDELL PHILLIPS

THE COMMITMENT

**Doubt who you will,
but never yourself.**

—CHRISTINE BOVEE

◇

**He who has a why to live for
can bear with almost any how.**

—FRIEDRICH NIETZSCHE

◇

**Perhaps I am
stronger than I think.**

—THOMAS MERTON

Show me someone who has done something worthwhile, and I'll show you someone who has overcome adversity.

—LOU HOLTZ

◇

I am not concerned that you have fallen; I am concerned that you arise.

—ABRAHAM LINCOLN

◇

I encourage my students never to give up on their dream, to emulate effort above all, and to mix passion with discipline so as to make the most of luck when it strikes.

—DAVID PHILLIPS

THE COMMITMENT

THE ATTITUDE

Attitudes are habits of thought that predict or perpetuate our performance. We aren't born with them—they are acquired. Notice that the most interesting and successful people have acquired the habit of talking about what they are for rather than what they are against.

To make headway, improve your head.

—B.C. FORBES

Their optimism pulls and propels them forward. They lean *into* life rather than away from it. How about you? Do you see difficulties behind every opportunity, or opportunities behind every difficulty?

Everything can be taken from man except the last of the human freedoms, his ability to choose his own attitude in any given set of circumstances—to choose his own way.

—VICTOR FRANKL

◇

**It is neither good nor bad,
but thinking makes it so.**

—WILLIAM SHAKESPEARE

◇

**We cannot tell what may happen
to us in the strange medley of life.
But we can decide what happens in us,
how we take it, what we do with it—
and that is what really counts in the end.**

—JOSEPH FORT NEWTON

THE ATTITUDE

Pain is inevitable; suffering is optional.
—Dr. H. Witte

◇

Your mind can focus on fear,
worry, problems, negativity or despair.
Or it can focus on confidence,
opportunity, solutions, optimism
and success. You decide.
—Don Ward

◇

When one door closes another door
opens; but we often look so longingly
and so regretfully upon the door that
closed, that we fail to see the one that
has opened for us.
—Helen Keller

THE ATTITUDE

Losers always have an excuse;
Winners always have an idea.
Losers fix the blame;
Winners fix the situation.
Losers make promises;
Winners keep commitments.
Losers let it happen;
Winners make it happen.
Losers say, "Why don't they do
something?" Winners say,
"Here's something I can do."

—EDGE KEYNOTE

◇

Attitudes are contagious.
Do you want people around you
to catch yours?

—BOB MOAWAD

THE ATTITUDE

Give your positive emotions a job.

—RALPH M. FORD

◇

I realize that a sense of humor isn't for
everyone. It's only for people who want
to have fun, enjoy life, and feel alive.

—ANNE WILSON SCHAEF

◇

Are you paying too much
attention to minor irritations?
Life is too short to be little.

—EDGE KEYNOTE

THE ATTITUDE

**Don't lose your head.
It's the best part of your body.**

—JIMMY SNYDER

◆

**If you're anticipating the worst while
hoping for the best, you will usually get
the worst. Turn it around! Imagine
the best, expect the best—and you'll
usually get the best.**

—DAN ZADRA

◆

**"I must do something"
will always solve more problems
than "Something must be done."**

—BITS & PIECES

THE ATTITUDE

Some favorite expressions of small
children: "It's not my fault...They made
me do it...I forgot." Some favorite expressions of small adults: "It's not my job...
No one told me...It couldn't be helped."
True freedom begins and ends with
personal accountability.

—DAN ZADRA

◆

Winners believe in their worth
in advance of their performance.

—DENIS WAITLEY

◆

When building a team, always look for
people who love to win. If you can't find any
of those, search for people who hate to lose.

—ROSS PEROT

THE ATTITUDE

They can because they think they can.

—VERGIL, THE AENEID

◆

**Be absolutely determined
to enjoy what you do.**

—GERRY SIKORSKI

◆

**The happiest people seem to be those
who have no particular cause for being
happy except that they are so.**

—WILLIAM RALPH INGE

THE DRIVE

We all get 24 hours a day. It's the only fair thing; it's the only thing that's equal. It's up to us to determine what we do with those 24 hours. We can waste them, or we can choose to consistently fill them with good.

All things come to those who go after them.

—ROB ESTES

Preparation, practice, hustle, grit, initiative and drive—these are all old-fashioned words, but they have built the world.

**What is it going to be—
reasons or results?**

—ART TUROCK

◇

**You can't make footprints
in the sands of time if you're sitting
on your butt. And who wants to make
buttprints in the sands of time?**

—BOB MOAWAD

◇

**Spectacular achievement is always
preceded by spectacular preparation.**

—DR. ROBERT SCHULLER

**If I just work when the spirit
moves me, the spirit will ignore me.**

—CAROLYN FORCHE

◇

**Beethoven, Wagner, Bach and
Mozart all worked regular shifts each
day, just like an accountant settles in at
the computer. They did not sit down to
work because they were inspired, but
became inspired because they sat
down to work.**

◇

**I hated every minute of the training,
but I said, "Don't quit. Suffer now and
live the rest of your life as a champion."**

—MUHAMMAD ALI

I see no virtue where I smell no sweat.

—FRANCIS QUARLES

◇

To every person there comes that special moment when he is tapped on the shoulder to do a very special thing unique to him. What a tragedy if that moment finds him unprepared for the work that would be his finest hour.

—WINSTON CHURCHILL

◇

We say we waste time, but that is impossible. We waste ourselves.

—ALICE BLOCH

THE DRIVE

Prepare! The time will come
when winter will ask what you
were doing all summer.

—HENRY CLAY

◇

No one has ever drowned
in his own sweat.

—D. H. THOMAS

◇

One of life's most painful
moments comes when we must
admit that we didn't do our homework,
that we are not prepared.

—MERLIN OLSEN

THE DRIVE

**When you're not practicing,
remember that someone somewhere
is practicing, and when you meet
him he will win.**

—ED MACAULEY

◇

**Tears will get you sympathy.
Sweat will get you change.**

—JESSE JACKSON

◇

**Life's most persistent and
urgent question is: What are you
doing for others?**

—MARTIN LUTHER KING, JR.

THE DRIVE

The best way out is always through.

—ROBERT FROST

◇

**The harder you work,
the harder it is to surrender.**

—VINCE LOMBARDI

◇

**We can redeem anyone who
strives unceasingly.**

—GOETHE

**I've never lost a game in my life.
Once in a while, time ran out on me.**

—BOBBY LAYNE, NFL QUARTERBACK

◇

**When you put a limit on what
you will do, you have put a limit on
what you can do.**

—CHARLES SCHWAB

◇

**When you have done your best,
await the result in peace.**

—EDGE KEYNOTE

THE ESTEEM

From the time we are little children, we are reminded to "Love our neighbors as ourselves," and the interesting thing is, *we always do!* To determine the degree to which individuals like and respect them-selves, simply watch the way they treat the people around them.

Don't forget to love yourself.

—SOREN KIERKEGAAR

Consideration, thoughtfulness, integrity, candor, character and class—these are all distinguishing characteristics of people wit sound self-esteem; the people we love, respect, follow and adm

**People who matter are most
aware that everyone else does, too.**

—MALCOLM FORBES

◇

**People with humility don't think
less of themselves—they just think
about themselves less.**

—KEN BLANCHARD

◇

**Each day silently affirm
that you are the type of person with
whom you would like to spend
the rest of your life.**

—BOB MOAWAD

THE ESTEEM

Have unconditional warm regards for all people at all times. Treat everyone, including and especially yourself, with consideration and respect.

—EDGE KEYNOTE

◇

If you're too busy to help the people around you succeed, you're too busy.

—BOB MOAWAD

◇

If you insist on measuring yourself, put the tape around your heart rather than your head. Try measuring your wealth by who you are, rather than what you have.

—CAROL TRABELLE

THE ESTEEM

**Whenever you are to do a thing,
though it can never be known but to
yourself, ask yourself how you would
act were all the world looking at you,
and act accordingly.**

—THOMAS JEFFERSON

◇

**We must have good domestic relations
with ourselves before we can have good
foreign relations with others.**

—RABBI JOSHUA LOTHLIEBMAN

◇

**Those you followed passionately, gladly
and zealously have made you feel like
somebody. It wasn't merely the job title
or power—they somehow made you feel
terrific to be around them.**

—IRWIN FEDERMAN

THE ESTEEM

If you don't place a high value on your talents, who will? If you don't think highly of yourself, why would anyone?

—EDGE KEYNOTE

◇

People are in greater need of your praise when they try and fail, than when they try and succeed.

—BOB MOAWAD

◇

Accept compliments easily and share your successes with others who have contributed to them. No one ever goes alone to the heights of excellence.

—EDGE KEYNOTE

THE ESTEEM

To be truly free and to grow in
self-esteem, choose not to give up your
growth, pursuit of fulfillment or happiness
to anyone. Choose to treat yourself with
dignity and proceed to move toward full
love, wisdom, freedom and joy, knowing
that y*ou* are the authority over *you.*

—LILBURN BARKSDALE

◇

No one can make you feel inferior
without your consent.

—ELEANOR ROOSEVELT

◇

Everyone appreciates being appreciated.
Catch people red-handed in the act
of doing something right each day—
and praise them for it.

—BOB MOAWAD

THE ESTEEM

It's the greatest compliment to be humble. You want to be the best you can be, but not compare yourself with others. I'd just like to be seen as someone maximizing my own talents.

—HAKEEM OLAJUWON

◇

Character is what you are in the dark.

—DWIGHT L. MOODY

◇

Have the courage to say no. Have the courage to face the truth. Do the right thing because it is right. These are the magic keys to living your life with integrity.

—W. CLEMENT STONE

THE ESTEEM

Love cures people—
both the ones who give it and
the ones who receive it.
—DR. CARL MENNINGER

◇

They are strong who can laugh
at themselves and cry for others.
—KOBI YAMADA

◇

Know you're good, wear it well
and share it with others. Self-esteem
is the degree to which you like and
respect yourself and feel confident
in dealing with life's challenges.

—EDGE KEYNOTE

THE ESTEEM

THE EDGE

The difference between the bottom and the top, between success and failure, between mediocrity and excellence, is often very small. A single insight is sometimes worth a life's experience. The accumulation of a lot of little things isn't little. So breathe in experience. Remain a lifelong learner. Fine-tune your skills and sweat the details. Constantly be on the look-out for the little difference that can make a big difference.

It's what you learn after you know it all that cou[nts]

—A. C. CARLSON

**Those who think they know it all
have no way of finding out they don't.**

—LEO BUSCAGLIA

◇

**Education consists mainly
in what we have unlearned.**

—MARK TWAIN

◇

**If at first you don't succeed,
before you try again, stop to figure
out what you did wrong.**

—LEO ROSTEN

You can work at something
for twenty years and come away
with twenty years worth of valuable
experience, or you can come away with
one year's experience twenty times.

—GWEN JACKSON

◇

Neil Eskelin watched in wonder
as a tiny ant struggled to carry a large
piece of straw. Blocked by a deep crack
in the ground, the ant carefully laid
the piece of straw across the gap and
walked to the other side. What
appeared to be a burden for the
ant was actually his freedom!

**Beware of those who
won't be bothered with details.**

—WILLIAM FEATHER

◇

**Don't just learn the tricks of the trade.
Learn the trade.**

—JAMES BENNIS

◇

**Focus on your natural strengths
and abilities. Exploit what you have,
not what you don't have.**

—ERIC OSSERMON

THE EDGE

Most ball games are lost, not won.

—CASEY STENGEL

◇

**Winners have simply formed the habit
of doing things losers don't like to do.**

—ALBERT GRAY

◇

**Everybody has to try
just a little bit harder, do just a little
bit better, think just a little deeper,
work just a little longer.**

—MARY LOU RETTON

THE EDGE

The fifty-goal scorer sees the back of the net; the five-goal scorer can tell you the brand name of the pads on every goalie in the league.

—WAYNE GRETZKY, PRO HOCKEY PLAYER

◇

Inches make champions.

—VINCE LOMBARDI

◇

There is greatness all around you— use it. It is easy to be great when you get around great people.

—BOB RICHARDS

THE EDGE

It's not the amount of time
you devote, but what you devote
to the time that counts.

—EDGE KEYNOTE

◆

Oh, the difference between
nearly right and exactly right.

—HORACE J. BROWN

◆

In order to succeed,
at times you have to make
something from nothing.

—RUTH MICKLEBY-LAND

In a time of drastic change, it is the learner who will inherit the future.

—ERIC HOFFER

◇

You will never "find" time for anything. If you want time, you must make it.

—CHARLES BUXTON

◇

When you have exhausted all possibilities, remember this—you haven't.

—EDGE KEYNOTE

THE STANDARDS

It's a competitive world out there, with each of us contributing something new and, hopefully, better to it. Every day, in every little corner of that world, some-one somewhere is pushing the quality of their product, service

Good enough never is.

—DEBBI FIELDS

or work—their standards—a little higher, a little closer to the heights of excellence. Set your own standards, but be inspired by the work of others. Continuously learn from it. Build on it. Challenge it. Surpass it!

**Nobody knows what is
the best he can do.**

—ARTURO TOSCANINI

◇

**Excellence is not a spectator sport.
Everyone's involved.**

—GENERAL ELECTRIC

◇

**First we will be best, and then
we will be first.**

—COMPENDIUM, INC.

THE STANDARDS

A competitive world offers
two possibilities. You can lose.
Or, if you want to win,
you can change.

—L.C. THUROW

◇

Be grateful for competition.
When your competitors upset your
plans or outdo your designs, they
open the infinite possibilities of
your own work to you.

—GIL ATKINSON

◇

Ruthlessly compete with your
own best self.

—APOLLO 13 ENGINEERS

Continuous improvement is impossible without continuous innovation.

—DON GALER

◇

Almost means not quite. Not quite means not right. Not right means wrong. Wrong means the opportunity to start again and get it right.

—DAN ZADRA

◇

Do it. Do it right. Do it right now.

—NASA SLOGAN

THE STANDARDS

**If you keep doing what
you've always done, you'll keep
getting what you've always got...
if you're fortunate.**
—BOB MOAWAD

◇

**Someone once asked me if there
wasn't benefit in overlooking one
small flaw. "What is a small flaw?"
I asked him.**
—DON SHULA

◇

**Hold yourself responsible for a higher
standard than anybody else expects of
you. Never excuse yourself.**
—HENRY WARD BEECHER

Who wants to be average?
Average is that place in the middle.
It's the best of the worst, or the
worst of the best.

—BOB MOAWAD

◇

I could use a hundred people
who don't know there is such a word
as impossible.

—HENRY FORD

◇

Impossible only defines
the degree of difficulty.

—DAVID PHILLIPS

THE STANDARDS

**Those who stop
being better stop being good.**

—OLIVER CROMWELL

◇

**People who are resting on
their laurels are wearing them
on the wrong end.**

—MALCOLM KUSHNER

◇

**Never mistake goodwill
for the deed.**

—FRANK VIZARRE

**If what you did yesterday
seems big, you haven't done
anything today.**

—LOU HOLTZ

◇

Growth is the only evidence of life.

—CARDINAL NEWMAN

◇

**If you won't be better
tomorrow than you were today, then
what do you need tomorrow for?**

—RABBI NAHMAN OF BRATSLAV

THOUGHTS
FOR THE ROAD

Eleanor Roosevelt loved to say that the future belongs to those who believe in the beauty of their dreams. In the long run, we really do shape our own lives; and then together we shape the world around us. The process

Good news! Most of our future lies ahead.
—DENNY CRUM

never ends until we die, and the choices we make are ultimately our responsibility. So choose wisely, boldly and confidently. Believe that your choices make a difference—they do!—and enjoy these final thoughts to accompany you on the journey. Here's to you—and to excellence in all that you do.

Remember that you are unique.
If that is not fulfilled, then something
wonderful has been lost.

—MARTHA GRAHAM

◇

It is never too late to be what
you might have been.

—GEORGE ELIOT

◇

Don't let anyone steal your dream.
It's your dream, not theirs.

—DAN ZADRA

THOUGHTS FOR THE ROAD

**Never compromise yourself.
You are all you've got.**

—BETTY FORD

◇

**There are only two things you
"have to" do in life. You "have to" die
and you "have to" live until you die.
You make up all the rest.**

—MARILYN GREY

◇

**What people say you cannot do,
you try and find that you can.**

—THOREAU

**Never place a period
where God has placed a comma.**

—GRACIE ALLEN

◇

**Realize that nothing is
too good to be true.**

—KOBI YAMADA

◇

**Some things have to be believed
to be seen.**

—RALPH HODGSON

No matter what the statistics say, there's always a way.

—BERNARD SIEGEL

◇

Be assured that you'll always have time for the things you put first.

—LIANE STEELE

◇

Don't just live the length of your life— live the width of it as well.

—DIANE ACKERMAN

**Plead guilty and often to
loving your family and friends.**

—DAN ZADRA

◇

**Remember that what is hard
to endure will be sweet to recall.**

—TOTE YAMADA

◇

**It is good to have an end to
journey towards—but it is the journey
that matters, in the end.**

—URSULA K. LeGUIN

Keep a diary of your daily wins
and accomplishments. If your life is
worth living, it's worth recording.

—MARILYN GREY

❖

None of us can go it alone.
Support your team.

—DR. ROBERT SCHULLER

❖

Learn from the mistakes
of others. You can't live long enough
to make them all yourself.

—CARLYLE

THOUGHTS FOR THE ROAD

Be assured that most of
your problems will disappear by
themselves if you don't get too
attached to them.

—EDGE KEYNOTE

◇

What appears to be the end of the road
may simply be a bend in the road.

—DR. ROBERT SCHULLER

◇

If your horse dies, get off.

—ANONYMOUS

THOUGHTS FOR THE ROAD

There will be ebbs and flows.
Remember that the tide always
always comes back.

—KEEP ON KEEPIN' ON

◇

Always know in your heart that
you are far bigger than anything
that can happen to you.

—DAN ZADRA

◇

If you're already walking on
thin ice, why not dance?

—GIL ATKINSON

THOUGHTS FOR THE ROAD

Forever remember that the business of life is not merely about business, but about life.

—B. C. FORBES

◇

Many of the things you can count, don't count. Many of the things you can't count, really count.

—ALBERT EINSTEIN

◇

Love people. Use things. Not vice-versa.

—KELLY ANN ROTHAUS

When you grow old or ill, the most important things to you will be who and what you've loved.

—JUNE MARTIN

◇

Never think you've seen the last of anything.

—EUDORA WELTY

◇

As you get older, don't slow down, speed up. There's less time left.

—MALCOLM FORBES

THOUGHTS FOR THE ROAD

When the grass appears greener
on the other side of the fence...
fertilize your grass.

—EDGE KEYNOTE

◇

Never let yesterday
use up too much of today.

—KOBI YAMADA

◇

There are only so many tomorrows.

—MICHAEL LANDON

THOUGHTS FOR THE ROAD

**Be gentle and patient
with people. Everyone's bruised.**

—KATIE LAMBERT

◇

**If you want love, give it away.
If you want friends, be one.
That's how it works.**

—DAN ZADRA

◇

**Hold a true friend with
both your hands.**

—AFRICAN PROVERB

THOUGHTS FOR THE ROAD

**Live each and every day
as if it were your last—because
one day you'll be right.**

—BOB MOAWAD

◇

**You have not lived a perfect
day unless you've done something
for someone who will never be
able to repay you.**

—RUTH SMELTZER

◇

**You never know when
you're making a memory.**

—RICKIE LEE JONES

THOUGHTS FOR THE ROAD

**You can't have everything—
where would you put it?**

—ANONYMOUS

◇

**Be good to yourself.
If you don't take care of your body,
where will you live?**

—KOBI YAMADA

◇

**For all that has been, Thanks.
For all that will be, Yes.**

—DAG HAMMARSKJOLD

THOUGHTS FOR THE ROAD

**Savor life's tiny delights—
a crackling fire, a glorious sunset,
a hug from a child, a walk with a
friend, a kiss behind the ear.**

—JOHN ANTHONY

◇

**If you don't have all the things you
want, be grateful for all the things you
don't have that you didn't want.**

—GIL ATKINSON

◇

He who laughs, lasts.

—MARY PETTIBONE POOLE

THOUGHTS FOR THE ROAD

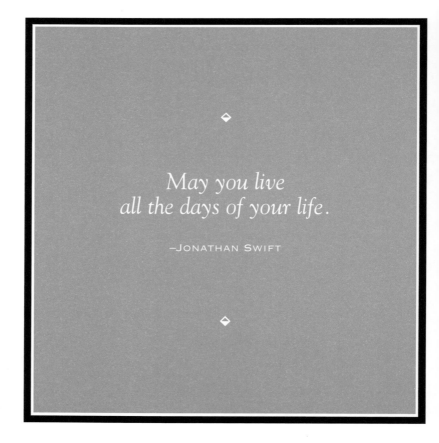

May you live
all the days of your life.

–JONATHAN SWIFT

GIVE THE WORLD YOUR BEST

———◇———

People are illogical, unreasonable and self-centered.
Love them anyway.

If you do good, people will accuse you of
selfish ulterior motives.
Do good anyway.

If you are successful, you win false friends and true enemies.
Succeed anyway.

The good you do today will be forgotten tomorrow.
Do good anyway.

Honesty and frankness will make you vulnerable.
Be honest and frank anyway.

The biggest people with the biggest ideas can be shot down
by the smallest people with the smallest minds.
Think big anyway.

What you spend years building may be destroyed overnight.
Continue to build anyway.

People really need help, but may attack you if you do help them.
Help them anyway.

Give the world the best you have and you may get kicked in the teeth.
Give the world the best you have anyway.

Also available from Compendium Publishing are these spirited and compelling companion books of great quotations.

Because of You™
Celebrating the Difference You Make™
Thoughts to inspire the people who inspire us™

Brilliance™
Uncommon Voices From Uncommon Women™
Thoughts to Inspire and Celebrate Your Achievements™

Forever Remembered™
A Gift for the Grieving Heart™
*Cherished messages of hope, love and comfort from
courageous people who have lost a loved one™*

Little Miracles™
To renew your dreams, lift your spirits, and strengthen your resolve™
Cherished messages of hope, joy, love, kindness and courage™

To Your Success™
Dream • Team • Care • Dare™
Thoughts to give wings to your work and your dreams™

You've Got a Friend™
Thoughts to Celebrate the Joy of Friendship™

*These books may be ordered directly form the publisher (800) 914-3327.
But please try your bookstore first!*